STEVE WATERS

Steve Waters' plays include *Temple* (Donmar Warehouse); *Why Can't We Live Together?* (Menagerie Theatre/Soho/Theatre503); *Europa*, as co-author (Birmingham Repertory Theatre/Dresden State Theatre/Teatr Polski Bydgoszcz/Zagreb Youth Theatre); *Ignorance/Jahiliyyah* (Hampstead Downstairs); *Little Platoons*, *The Contingency Plan*, *Capernaum* (part of *Sixty-Six Books*; Bush, London); *Fast Labour* (Hampstead, in association with West Yorkshire Playhouse); *Out of Your Knowledge* (Menagerie Theatre/Pleasance, Edinburgh/East Anglian tour); *World Music* (Sheffield Crucible, and subsequent transfer to the Donmar Warehouse); *The Unthinkable* (Sheffield Crucible); *English Journeys*, *After the Gods* (Hampstead); a translation/adaptation of a new play by Philippe Minyana, *Habitats* (Gate, London/ Tron, Glasgow); *Flight Without End* (LAMDA). Writing for television and radio includes *Safe House* (BBC4), *The Air Gap*, *The Moderniser* (BBC Radio 4), *Scribblers* and *Bretton Woods* (BBC Radio 3). Steve ran the Birmingham MPhil in Playwriting between 2006 and 2011 and now runs the MA Creative Writing: Script at the University of East Anglia. He is the author of *The Secret Life of Plays*, also published by Nick Hern Books.

Other Titles in this Series

Steve Waters

LIMEHOUSE

NICK HERN BOOKS
London
www.nickhernbooks.co.uk

A Nick Hern Book

Limehouse first published in Great Britain in 2017 as a paperback original by Nick Hern Books Limited, The Glasshouse, 49a Goldhawk Road, London W12 8QP

Limehouse copyright © 2017 Steve Waters

Steve Waters has asserted his moral right to be identified as the author of this work

Cover photograph: *Telegraph*

Designed and typeset by Nick Hern Books, London
Printed in Great Britain by CPI Group (UK) Ltd

A CIP catalogue record for this book is available from the British Library

ISBN   978 1 84842 642 9

This play is dedicated to the memory of my mother,
Yvonne June Waters, 1941–2016;
and also to the memory of
Howard Davies, 1945–2016.

Acknowledgements

The author would like to thank the following people for their assistance in the writing of the play:

Professor Michael Kenny, Lord Roger Liddle, Lord David Owen, Lady Debbie Owen, Lord Bill Rodgers, Baroness Shirley Williams.

None of the opinions in the play are attributable to them.

Thanks too to Polly Findlay, Josie Rourke, Clare Slater, the cast of the original production and all the Donmar Warehouse for their assistance in the development of the play.

S.W.

Limehouse was first performed at the Donmar Warehouse, London, on 8 March 2017 (previews from 2 March), with the following cast, in order of speaking:

DEBBIE OWEN	Nathalie Armin
DAVID OWEN	Tom Goodman-Hill
BILL RODGERS	Paul Chahidi
SHIRLEY WILLIAMS	Debra Gillett
ROY JENKINS	Roger Allam

Director	Polly Findlay
Designer	Alex Eales
Lighting Designer	Jon Clark
Sound Designer	Emma Laxton
Composer	Rupert Cross
Casting Director	Alastair Coomer CDG

Limehouse is a fictionalised account of real events. It is not endorsed by the individuals portrayed.

'In Limehouse, in Limehouse, before the break of day,
I hear the feet of many men who go upon their way,
Who wander through the City,
The grey and cruel City,
The streets where men decay.'

Clement Attlee, 1912

'The plural of conscience is conspiracy'

Arthur Henderson

Characters

DAVID OWEN, *Labour MP – forty-two*
DEBBIE OWEN, *American, literary agent, David's wife –*
    thirty-eight
BILL RODGERS, *Labour MP – fifty-two*
SHIRLEY WILLIAMS, *ex-Labour MP – fifty*
ROY JENKINS, *ex-Labour politician and President of the*
    European Commission – sixty

Setting

The Owens' house, Narrow Street, Limehouse, London,
January 25th, 1981.

This play is a fiction based on real events.

This text went to press before the end of rehearsals and so may
differ slightly from the play as performed.

One

Early morning. The Owens' kitchen.

A cork-tiled floor; the walls are painted white. Reclaimed-wood kitchen units stage left with sink; gas-hob cooker to the rear; stylish but not fancy; the wooden surfaces hold a plate rack and stacked plates; pots of herbs and flowers. From overhead beams hang drying herbs and implements. In the centre of the stage is a large round table of planed oak, rough and uneven; around it elegant wooden chairs, documents, papers; basket of fruit. It feels oddly timeless and handmade, comfortable and chic.

Light comes in from street lights from the front; to the rear two doors upstage-left and right to an open-plan living space, with large picture windows revealing the sky and the open expanse of the Thames looking south to Rotherhithe; stage right leads to a staircase down to the street and telephone; stage left into the rest of the house and children's rooms upstairs.

It's four in the morning; moonlight, cold and pitiless through the high windows, meets the sodium glow from the street.

DEBBIE OWEN *enters in a dressing gown.*

DEBBIE *speaks to the audience.*

DEBBIE. When I was a child we used to summer on Long Island,

the sound of tidal shifts and the snapping of sails in the breeze sang me to sleep,

and here in Limehouse, you wake and sleep to the river's shift and pull, the barges out at anchor on the Thames or the collier's boat knocking at the jetty; all day long the river shifts and swells, smacking at our windows like it's signalling something

and that day in January, 1981, it felt like history was a surge beating at the doors and calling us,

calling us out.

DAVID OWEN *enters – he's in yesterday's clothes*.

DAVID. We have to start again.

DEBBIE. You need to sleep.

I need to sleep.

DAVID. I should call up somebody, Peter at the *Guardian*, yes, I'll just call Peter up.

DEBBIE. At 4 a.m.? You think he's waiting up for you? To say what exactly?

DAVID. Up with this we may no longer put! No more fudge and mudge!

DEBBIE. I suspect that can wait on Monday. And please keep your voice down, you'll wake the children.

DAVID. Yesterday, in full public view the Labour Party committed hara-kiri. So why are the others so slow in instinct? Surely they know it's kill or cure from now on.

DEBBIE. Okay, so we're discussing this now.

DAVID. Obviously we're discussing this now, yes.

DEBBIE. Look, tomorrow – today's – Sunday, can't you maybe, I don't know put out some sort of press statement: 'Coming soon, "Great Events"'; I could rustle something up for you – come the morning –

DAVID. The printer's rollers are turning, the ink's hot, the last copy from the columnists's in – right this minute, Labour's obituary's being typed – forget the motions and manifestos, there's one story from conference: the Hard Left are in the driving seat – hot-wired the party, the unions, gerrymandered the leadership vote – and now we no longer say who leads us, no longer own the policies we go to the country with – and Monday morning every paper in the land will print that story. We have a day to stop that happening.

DEBBIE. Okay, yes, okay. I do see that, I do – get that.

DAVID. Well, thank God I'm not the only one who does.

Pause.

DEBBIE. Isn't Roy with you? He's looking for a job, isn't he, now Europe's done with, he must be pretty desperate.

DAVID. Desperate for this to be the Roy Jenkins show. No one knows where Roy stands, but if he leads us we're sunk before we're out the port, the man's a relic, a decade past his sell-by date.

DEBBIE. Sure, sure – but Bill Rodgers's onside, right, he's pretty discontent.

DAVID. Oh Bill's Roy's poodle, does his bidding, runs his errands, when he's not doubling as Shirley's mascot; makes all the noises but hasn't got the bloody attack.

DEBBIE. So Shirley's the real prize?

DAVID. Not an MP right now, not got the guts for this fight, impossible to pin down.

DEBBIE. Well, correct me if I'm wrong but you can't create a party on your own.

DAVID. Of course I *fucking* can't.

A young child calls off. They wince, wait.

A tugboat's lights and the sound of a horn through fog.

The crying stops.

Another working breakfast at Bill's then, hand-wringing and open letters; tomorrow we'll be a laughing stock.

Better start looking at the vacancies in the BMJ.

DEBBIE. No! No, you don't go back to that – you haven't even begun in this, in politics – this is your chance, your time to make something genuinely you, genuinely new.

DAVID. Bill thinks I'm a wrecker, Shirley thinks I'm a lightweight, Roy thinks I'm Oswald Moseley –

DEBBIE. David, remember first and foremost you're all friends.

DAVID. There's no friendship in politics.

Pause.

DEBBIE. So treat them as friends.

Why do you never meet here?

DAVID. They don't trust me to host! I'm the outlier.

DEBBIE. So, okay, get them over.

Build that trust. Let them see you like this.

DAVID. To what end?

No, they'll instantly smell a rat.

And anyway you're having lunch with your client, aren't you?

DEBBIE. Absolutely, and the boys have football and it's the au pair's day off and I have three manuscripts to read, but all of that will have to wait.

We host tomorrow. No more frat parties at Bill's on gin and Marmite sandwiches or cold suppers at Shirley's or roast-beef lunches at Roy's. I'll cook up something… whatever we have in the house. Something convivial, warm, companionable – and we make it plain what you have between you – what you share.

And hold back on the papers, tip them off that something's coming, that by teatime they will have that something.

Pause.

DAVID. Christ. Okay.

DEBBIE. And we'll need to charm them and I know you don't do charm, but you need to show that you love and understand each one of them, and keep the gas low and if you do this by close of play I promise you you'll be more than a gang you'll be a party.

Honey?

DAVID. All right.

Good. Good.

Brilliant, actually.

DEBBIE. Yes?

DAVID. Quite brilliant.

Debbie – I am nothing without you.

Blackout.

In the dark a radio plays Alistair Cooke's Letter from
America *discussing, ponderously, the inauguration of
Ronald Reagan.*

Two

*9 a.m. Winter light streams in from the picture windows; foggy
haze.* BILL RODGERS, *in raincoat covering M&S sweater
and jeans; he holds a carrier bag with food.* DEBBIE *is making
a shopping list, weighing out pasta, rooting in the fridge for
cheese, noting it down.*

BILL. You're very far east.

Thought Kentish Town was off the map; this place is terra
incognita.

DEBBIE. We like to be away from the fray.

BILL. Certainly away from that.

Not the first idea how to get here; drove round and round Old
Street roundabout like *The Flying Dutchman,* forgot my *A to
Z,* thinking, 'just get on to Commercial Road'; luckily barely
a milk float in sight.

Seems there's less urgency than I feared.

Am I very early?

DEBBIE. Maybe you could fix some coffee – filter paper there,
coffee in the tin above the sink; David's dressing the
children, be right down – David!

BILL. Okay. Coffee sounds an excellent interim plan.

He readies the coffee.

Oh I salvaged some of what I laughably call lunch.

DEBBIE. Really no need to do that.

BILL. Just given we were meant to be hosting, not that I'm making a thing of it, just all a little… sudden.

DEBBIE. It felt like maybe it was our turn – and we have the space as you see and well, the advantage of being out on a limb.

BILL. No complaints about the venue, Debbie; far more chic than chez Rodgers.

Yes, just some rather whiffy camembert, somewhat leaky and shall we say – whew – high –

DEBBIE. Ooh – yes, that's certainly ripe –

She's at the fridge.

Oh, bottle of something to warm us all up on the side there.

BILL. Ah, yes. Château Lafite? My word, no expense spared.

DEBBIE. Figured we ought to maintain his standards.

BILL. Uncanny – the Lafite's his tipple of choice. *Le Roi Jean Quinze* will be chuffed.

DEBBIE. Excuse me?

BILL. Oh. What they call Roy. In Brussels.

Le Roi Jean Quinze.

Somewhat laboured joke.

DEBBIE. I guess my French is a little rusty.

BILL. Of course; it's – Le Roi – 'Roy', of course, and 'king' – gosh this *is* very laboured. Anyway, what passes for humour in Belgium.

DEBBIE. Coffee good to go?

BILL. Yes, yes, just fit this filter in – dispense with the incumbent – there.

DEBBIE. David, Bill's here!

BILL. Mortifyingly early. But he did say early.

DEBBIE. Hell of a night here – hope we didn't wake you –

BILL. Not really sleeping, right now.

Crazy febrile dreams – oh – was I being sat on by – was it Tony Benn? Pipe in mouth, sitting atop me like I was some sort of chaise longue.

DEBBIE. No call for Freud there!

BILL. Not really. David didn't sleep you say?

DEBBIE. Oh… y'know, just the whole – excitement.

BILL. Certainly seemed – excitable – yesterday. Roving conference like some great predator putting the wind up a pack of wildebeests. Had me flinching.

DEBBIE. David said you were magnificent. You know how highly he esteems you?

BILL. I don't garner esteem by and large.

Now coffee coming up…

DEBBIE. He always says Bill Rodgers's the only one of us who has the respect of the northern party.

Now could you open that and let it breathe a little?

She hands him a bottle and he grapples with it.

BILL. Bit premature for that.

DEBBIE. Not on a day like today.

Yes, he says 'No one works a room like Bill Rodgers'.

BILL. Kind words – for an – ailing apparatchnik like me –

He's struggling to open the bottle.

There – oof – sorry – oh dear –

BILL *waves and smiles through considerable pain; he is suddenly bent double.*

DEBBIE. Gosh, Bill, are you okay?

BILL. Just my – my – bloody back – actually, do you mind if I –

He descends painfully slowly to the floor.

Absolutely – fucking – (sorry) – crucifying me.

DEBBIE. Is it maybe lumbago? Sciatica?

BILL. Everyone says it's psychosomatic but if it is, it's extremely painfully – psychosomatic.

DAVID *comes in.*

DAVID. Lucy changed, powdered and dry as a bone.

Great, Bill, good and prompt.

BILL. Morning, David.

DAVID. Why are you down there?

DEBBIE. So Bill's back's playing up.

DAVID. Coffee, terrific.

DEBBIE. Oh, do you know we may have some 'deep heat'.

BILL. Driving exacerbates it, hunched over the wheel like that chap – Columbo.

DEBBIE. So we don't have any leeks. I'll pop out and see if they –

BILL. Well, why don't I do that?

DAVID. Sure they're necessary? The children are being picked up for ten, Tris's boots need re-studding.

DEBBIE. Doubt I'll be five minutes –

BILL *gets up, shakes out his back.*

BILL. I could get the papers too.

DAVID. No, we stay put; Chatham House rule. No leaking, no briefing, no pre-empting our great surprise.

BILL. Right. And what surprise is that?

DEBBIE. David struggles to distinguish between a request and an instruction.

DAVID. Gareth's creating some mighty fracas about his helicopter. Should we put Lucy down for her nap or will Sally want her wakeful?

DEBBIE. Sure, nap, yes. Oh, boil up the water whilst I'm gone. Pasta's just in the scales.

She goes.

DAVID. Dose up on paracetamol – make merry, doctor's orders.

I'll pump you out if you OD.

DAVID *laughs sharply, makes himself coffee.* BILL *takes his pills.*

BILL. Surprised Shirley's not here.

DAVID. Yah. Called her just after you.

BILL. Right.

DAVID. That all right?

BILL. Of course. Wasn't aware you had her number.

DAVID. You gave it me I think.

BILL. Did I?

Suppose she'll be here soon, belated and flustered.

DAVID. Roy should be with us around ten thirty.

BILL (*checks his little notebook*). Driving up from East Hendred.

You gave clear directions? He's used to being driven; Roy's not a natural navigator, I swear he gets lost in his own back garden. Mind you it's big enough.

DAVID. We've had him here before.

BILL. Wasn't that your other place?

DAVID. Oh. Keeping tabs on it, Bill?

BILL. I wouldn't say that, no.

DAVID. Well, you know him more intimately.

BILL. Mere foot soldier.

A moment.

DAVID. Reckon we can trust him?

In this endeavour, I mean?

BILL. Oh. Can we trust Roy?

Well; can you trust me?

DAVID. Don't be absurd, Bill, you're rock solid, you've led the way.

BILL. But can I trust you, David – if we're speaking of trust?

DAVID*'s buttering some coldish toast.*

DAVID. You must wonder what he wants, what he stands for now – out of the game, what, five years?

BILL. He's been very forthcoming on that.

DAVID. Is Roy ever forthcoming?

BILL. Well, breaking the mould of two-party politics, his bid for the Radical Centre.

DAVID. Oxymorons! Come-hither signals to the Liberal Party!

BILL. Sorry, David, not following your drift.

DAVID. The day we get in bed with that crowd of whimsical hobbyists – standing for nothing, standing up to nothing, frittering away their days on pisspot parish-council bickering – is the day I walk out on this – us.

He bites into the toast rather noisily.

Just to be absolutely clear on my stance; with regard to the Liberal Party.

BILL. Well, that's certainly clear.

But can we ignore eighteen per cent of the vote?

DAVID. Okay – this is where you are, is it?

BILL. Not sure I know what that means.

DAVID. Come on.

BILL. David, shouldn't we be waiting for the others before – ?

DAVID. The others aren't here.

Pause.

BILL. I don't disagree with you. With regard to the Liberals.

DAVID. No double negatives.

BILL. You're in a very insistent mood, if I may say.

DAVID. You sat with me through that eight-hour fuck-up
yesterday, poker-faced through Michael Foot waffling,
digressing, flannelling, flailing about, as we lost every vote
to the Marxist and Trots, but by close of play your head was
in your hands – where are you today, Bill?

DAVID *demolishes a banana.*

Milk? Sugar?

BILL (*nods*). What? Oh. Two, er, sugars.

DAVID. Now, and toast and I think we have brioche here.

BILL. Yes. Brioche sounds… nice. Mmm.

BILL *chews on a brioche. Yawns.*

Sorry. Didn't sleep a wink. Finally got off at three.

Woke with a start with this thought: what if there's a design
fault in the Labour Party?

I mean why else do we *always* hate our leaders?

Why this distaste for office as if power was somehow
a betrayal?

Why else would we spend most of our short life tearing
ourselves in two?

DAVID *joins him at the table.*

DAVID. All the way back: protest versus power; Left versus
Right.

BILL. Mmm.

Keir Hardie versus MacDonald.

DAVID. Lansbury versus Attlee.

BILL. Lansbury versus Bevin.

DAVID. Nye Bevan versus Attlee.

BILL. Bevan versus Gaitskell versus Wilson.

DAVID. Same fault line yesterday, Bill, the wound laid open, weeping – conference baying like a beast in the shambles – Jim and Denis and Shirley up there and you and me crammed in pens like this was Nuremberg and we were being bloody arraigned – the finger-jabbers and the clenched fists, the denouncers and the hate-mongers, Tony Benn smiling them on – yes, yes, deselect the right, scrap Trident, leave Europe, leave NATO, all by the weekend – Healey asleep at the wheel, Jim a broken reed, Michael waving his walking stick at the mob – it's so bloody clear to me today: it's *over*, Bill.

The only question is what we put in its place.

BILL *gets up*.

BILL. Yes, I think I'll go for a stroll.

Mmm. Take in the sights of Stepney – if there are any sights in Stepney.

Good for the back, right?

DAVID. The back's a symptom, Bill.

BILL. I see what you're doing here, David.

DAVID. You should get out of the Shadow Cabinet.

BILL. Right. As you did.

DAVID. Foot didn't even give you a portfolio. Worst of all worlds, neither in nor out.

BILL. I seem to recall you were more reluctant once.

DAVID. Well, when I go I ruddy well go!

You and Shirley seem to content to linger.

BILL (*putting on his coat*). Well, if I may say, you're not truly Labour, are you?

Not in your family, your blood.

My father was Labour. Municipal clerk on Liverpool council. Shirley's father failed to win a seat for Labour twice, he raised her to right that wrong, Roy's father was Attlee's PPS.

DAVID. Are we a fucking hereditary party now?

Look, take your coat off.

BILL. You see these are deep, deep things, David! And no, it's not very rational, and yes, I'm meant to be the rational one but I happen to be a loyalist too and I don't want to wake up in ten years' time and find Thatcher enthroned and Labour a bad memory. Sorry if that's disappointing to you.

DAVID. Well, I'm sorry but I can't let you go.

BILL. Right! I'd like to see you stop me.

DAVID. So Shirley will be here imminently –

BILL. You know that do you – ?

DAVID. Yes, and this is, what, a blocking tactic and worse than that it's not even civil –

BILL. Nevertheless it's what's happening.

DAVID. Bill, come on, sit down, I'll make another coffee.

BILL. No thanks, David – but thanks for the pain relief at least.

DAVID. Bill, for God's sake!

BILL*'s gone.*

Shit – bugger – shit.

Blackout.

Radio; the Morning Service; a hymn – 'Jerusalem' perhaps, sung in a dirge.

The water boils away. Phone rings; DAVID *goes.*

Three

10 a.m.

SHIRLEY WILLIAMS *in coat comes in with* DEBBIE. *We can hear* DAVID *shouting on the phone, off.* DEBBIE *goes to the cooker, checks the water, adds in the pasta. Unpacking food.*

SHIRLEY. Simply sat there seething, motion after motion. Actually a gasp when the vote came through, sheer disbelief. Of course Michael Foot said diddly-squat – lost the vote, nothing to say; and you sit up there on that platform, occupying a role you've largely been talked in to, surrounded by people who won't even be civil with you, and it's like you've been framed or something. How it must have felt in Moscow – at a show trial. When they started to sing 'The Red Flag' I couldn't bring myself to join in – I felt physically sick.

DEBBIE (*setting a timer*). No idea how you survive it all, frankly.

SHIRLEY. David was very good; sat on the steps, set out his stall; the union bosses had to literally step over him. The soul of truculence.

I envy you; having him, having your three.

Mind you, hard enough raising one.

Years of racing back from Cabinet to sing goodnight.

Do not venture there!

DEBBIE*'s now chopping an onion.*

DEBBIE. Apologies for any inadvertent tears.

SHIRLEY. Plenty to blub about.

I thought I was late. Where's Bill – he's usually on time?

DEBBIE. Yes, Bill was horribly prompt, bless him. I'm sure he's around somewhere.

SHIRLEY. Were they decrying my timekeeping? That incenses me; these men have nothing to detain them! Roy doesn't lift a finger, can't even peel an apple. Some of us happen to be single mothers. And getting here from Pimlico was anything but straightforward; why couldn't we meet in my flat?

DEBBIE. Oh, can I maybe get your coat?

SHIRLEY. I didn't bring anything for lunch. How thoughtless, let me just pop out –

DEBBIE. Lunch is taken care of.

And, and I'm instructed to keep you here.

DEBBIE *laughs*.

SHIRLEY. 'Instructed'?

DAVID *comes in with a toy helicopter.*

DAVID. Where's the Airfix glue? The very strong adhesive?

Ah, Shirley, wonderful.

SHIRLEY. In good time, I hope.

DEBBIE. Drawer on the right; next to the fridge.

She's now cutting up bacon.

SHIRLEY. Are you sure you're ready for us?

DAVID. Absolutely, of course.

SHIRLEY. Feels rather novel; being so punctual.

DEBBIE. Yes, and presumably everything's okay, David – I mean with Bill?

DAVID. Of course, Bill – yes, I think he probably just ran out to, er – to get the papers.

DEBBIE. So what, Bill's not here?

DAVID. That's right – for now. Besides isn't it good to shake things up a little, disrupt the usual cabals? I mean, do we ever talk without aides and intermediaries?

SHIRLEY. Bill's a little more than that.

DAVID. Ah, the killer glue – broken-propeller incident causing a diplomatic stand-off.

Did I claim a kiss from you?

SHIRLEY. Do you usually request?

DAVID. Fabulous to have you here at last –

　　DAVID *kisses her. Telephone rings.*

DEBBIE. Oh – the phone.

DAVID. Well, maybe you could –

DEBBIE. Right, okay, sure, I should – get that. (*Goes.*)

　　SHIRLEY *takes in the room,*

SHIRLEY. So the East End idyll we hear so much about – *rus in urbe*. You could almost walk out on to the river there.

　　Very you.

DAVID. Yes. Used to be a greasy spoon; ship captain's house you see, great corrugated metal boathouse at the back I oxyacetylaned off.

　　Can't think why we haven't got you over earlier.

SHIRLEY. Well, I rarely seem to socialise these days, except to plot in corridors. Not that I've ever been especially clubbable.

DAVID. We're alike in that respect.

SHIRLEY. Yes, I suppose we are; in that respect.

　　Pause.

DAVID. Okay, I'll say it right now as I have you alone, that whatever eventuates today you're the natural leader of it. And I don't say that to flatter, I say it out of cold calculation. You would be the ideal counter to Margaret; and I'd gladly stand behind you.

SHIRLEY. Crikey – David, hang on that's – utterly – *ridiculous* – that's – we're nowhere near decisions – decisions of this nature –

DAVID. This is your time! And I will back you to the hilt – and if you don't claim it we'll be lumbered with Roy, and Bill won't fight that and I think you know that.

SHIRLEY. I don't respond to flattery, I thought you knew me better than that, and I make my own decisions in my own time.

　　A moment.

DEBBIE (*re-enters*). David.

DAVID. What now?

DEBBIE. Oh – sorry, just it's – it's… Roy.

DAVID. We're busy here.

SHIRLEY. Are we?

DEBBIE. Just he's in a call box somewhere having difficulties and he's low in change.

DAVID. So what am I supposed to do about – ?

DEBBIE. Here's the number. He sounded quite – flustered. For Roy.

DAVID. Right, right. Better bloody get that then. (*Goes.*)

DEBBIE. You're still in your coat.

    DEBBIE *takes off* SHIRLEY*'s coat.*

SHIRLEY. Is David a bit of a bully to you, Debbie? Does he browbeat you?

DEBBIE. Gosh, do I look 'browbeaten'?

    Hey, I love the trouser suit.

SHIRLEY. Oh. Your honest opinion: is it a bit mutton?

DEBBIE. No. It's great fun – sporty.

    Pause.

    So there's plenty of coffee there, or I can do tea or herbals or –

SHIRLEY. Oh. Just a glass of cold water. I'll get it –

DEBBIE. Permit me to play house in my own house.

    DEBBIE *fetches it;* SHIRLEY *drinks it down in one. Doorbell.*

DAVID (*off*). Door.

SHIRLEY. Did I say it's super to meet you properly, Debbie?

DEBBIE. Oh likewise, likewise. I'm your greatest fan, you set such a great example: politically.

DAVID (*off*). On the latch.

SHIRLEY. Oh, enough of these silly fulsome blandishments.

DEBBIE. Actually I meant it in all sincerity.

   BILL *enters with papers*.

BILL. Bitter out there.

DEBBIE. You're back, Bill!

BILL. So it seems.

DEBBIE. I just mean that's got to be good news.

BILL. Have I been much missed?

DEBBIE. No – yes – you guys won't mind me doing some
   preparation… if it's not too disruptive.

SHIRLEY. We'll do that for you.

DEBBIE. No, you don't need to concern yourself –

BILL. More than happy to muck in.

SHIRLEY. Yes, presumably you need to tend to the little ones.

BILL. Right, chop up the leeks, right, fry this up – recipe there.

DEBBIE. Just, well, okay, so the bacon needs –

BILL. Bacon – right, I'm on bacon-prepping duties.

SHIRLEY. I'm a dab hand at chopping.

DEBBIE. Okay. Well, I guess it's in safe hands.

   DEBBIE *exits*.

BILL. Fashionably tardy as ever, Shirley.

SHIRLEY. Piss off, Bill, he said ten.

BILL. Said nine to me.

SHIRLEY. Did he – did he, indeed?

   What's the bloody hell is this all about?

BILL. Very good question.

   Take it you've seen these?

   He has the papers out.

SHIRLEY. Not had a moment; barely out of my nighty.

BILL. Have a shufty.

He fries the bacon. She leafs through the papers.

SHIRLEY. Plenty of coverage; the whole sorry shambles.

'The Gang of Four has twenty-four hours to act.'

BILL. Speak to anyone yesterday, did you?

SHIRLEY. No. No! Well, some junior on the *Observer* ambushed me at coffee; of course I said nothing.

BILL. As if our host's primed them. Boxing us in. Making this a *fait accomplit*. Look at *The Sunday Times*.

She roots it out.

Exclusive extracts from David Owen's personal manifesto: 'Face the Future'.

SHIRLEY. Did we know this – did he tell us?

BILL. Very convenient, don't you think, very timely certainly. Must have been cooking this up for some time; new book, new party, going for the Crosland crown; we're the chorus girls I suppose.

SHIRLEY. Bloody hell, look at that, all over, all over the shop, five whole pages: 'Face the Future'?

BILL. He likes his imperatives.

SHIRLEY. Even Lenin used the occasional question mark.

God – the absolute – flipping – cheek!

Is he appropriating us, Bill?

BILL. Looking like it.

We must keep schtum from now on.

SHIRLEY. Absolutely; although I do have a smallish interview at one – I think I did say.

BILL. Shirley – no! An interview? It's far too soon –

SHIRLEY. Just with the BBC.

BILL. The BBC?

SHIRLEY. Oh, only Radio 4.

BILL. *A propos* of what?

SHIRLEY. I don't know, probably just to reflect on events, on the conference, I don't know, wasn't aware I needed your permission.

BILL. You've not told them about today?

SHIRLEY. Nothing. Not a thing; Bill, don't look at me like that!

I remain absolutely wedded to the line that we change the party from within – publically.

BILL. Only publically?

The timer alarm goes. The pasta is boiling rather wildly.

SHIRLEY. Shouldn't we turn that off?

DEBBIE *comes in. She checks the pasta.*

DEBBIE. Rather al dente.

So David's sorry, he's likely to be a little longer.

BILL. What's he doing? I mean, doing what?

DEBBIE. Oh, just on the telephone, Bill.

SHIRLEY. To Roy.

BILL. Why on the earth would he be on the phone to Roy?

DEBBIE (*laughs*). Apparently he's lost in Shoreditch or environs.

Just give that stir. Nearly there.

A child is crying, off.

Oh heck.

She's restive today; didn't sleep through.

David!

DAVID (*off*). On the phone.

Doorbell.

DEBBIE. Oh great, Sally. Deliverance!

I'm usually quite an attentive mother.

I've an inkling that bacon's done.

BILL *switches off the gas*. DEBBIE *goes; during the next sequence the child goes quiet, some thundering down the stairs, goodbyes and the like*.

BILL. Okay.

So… we need to be quick.

SHIRLEY. Yes…

BILL. So our host is coming in hard for something decisive.

SHIRLEY. Yes. But about what?

BILL. Don't be coy.

SHIRLEY. You're the one being coy.

BILL. The putative new party.

SHIRLEY. The putative as yet non-existent party.

BILL. Yesterday put wind in his sails; the more dire things got, the more gleeful he became.

SHIRLEY. Yesterday was vile!

I can no longer be in a room with these people. Everyone's against me on the NEC – one by one the moderates taken out, disheartened, enfeebled; plain bullying too, my interventions blocked, tedious constitutional objections, constant filibustering – exactly what the fascists do, wear you down with your own weapons and then out come the coshes and castor oil; oh yes, they want me out of there, damned if I let them have their way, honestly I could, I could – *punch* them.

BILL. You're a vital presence on the NEC, Shirley; if you walk, that fight is utterly lost.

SHIRLEY. And where are you – today?

BILL. Much depends on Roy, of course.

SHIRLEY. Oh Bill, don't fling Roy at me, Roy's just a sideshow, this mustn't become another vehicle for his careerism.

BILL. He's being a little gnomic for sure.

SHIRLEY. Oh he loves being gnomic, suits him all too well, hardly lifted a finger on this – wafts in, expecting us to do his bidding, we do the heavy lifting, he gets the glory – you sentimentalise him, you know.

BILL. So, fine, what about you?

SHIRLEY. Ach – I can't stay and I can't go.

It's like when Bernard left me, almost as hard – except this time I'm the one going, and that feels wrong.

BILL. Well, okay but what if the party's left us?

SHIRLEY. The party! I earn not a penny from politics right now, and meanwhile I have Harvard offering me teaching, full relocation, not even an MP. I do wonder, if I've got the staying power.

BILL. For what?

SHIRLEY. For politics. Full stop.

Pause.

BILL. Shirley, no, you cannot walk away from this situation –

SHIRLEY. You didn't lose your seat, Bill – utterly shattering – just the ignominy.

BILL. '79 was a lottery, we deserved to be kicked out but ceding the field altogether is something else.

SHIRLEY. Thank God my parents were spared it. Drove home from the count in the dark, closed the curtains, slept like the dead – and when I awoke – God, such delicious, *delicious* freedom – I could actually be someone else, somebody other than fucking 'Shirley Williams MP'. Honestly, I was in the bath, splashing about like a baby, Saturday afternoon: forty-nine and free again.

BILL. This is no time for psychodramas.

SHIRLEY. Do I really want to put my head right back in the hive?

BILL. Shirley, I need hardly point to how unique you are – one of barely two women in Ministerial roles – who else – you, Barbara Castle –

SHIRLEY. Ellen Wilkinson, Jenny Lee –

BILL. You outstrip them in your achievement – what's Labour or what might replace it without you? Skulking on some American campus, that's a criminal waste of your talents – whether we leave or stay you will be critical.

SHIRLEY. All right, all right, Bill.

But if we go, it must be worth the pain it will cause to all of us.

BILL. Well, you know I won't if you don't.

SHIRLEY. Right.

We go together or we stay together.

Agreed?

They rather oddly shake hands; the timer rings again.

The Archers *theme plays.*

Four

11 a.m.

ROY JENKINS, *in a fine winter coat, gloves and scarf, stands in the midst of* BILL *washing some lettuce,* SHIRLEY *making salad dressing,* DAVID *laying the table,* DEBBIE *making a cheese sauce.*

ROY. An inspired change of venue, if an elusive one.

Driving here I could only think of the great Clement Attlee of whom it was said, 'Going East, he went Left'.

Sadly I then went left too and found myself in Mile End.

DAVID. Bit of a shock after Brussels I expect.

ROY. Oh a pleasant surprise, in fact.

Yes, wonderful properties of light and space here.

The least agreeable thing about Brussels is the perpetual Stygian gloom one's afflicted with; thirteen floors up, rarely sunlight of any quality.

I suspect we had not more than one day of continuous sunshine during my entire time as President. Constant crepuscular greyness; might as well have been in Pontypool.

Laughter except DAVID. DEBBIE *assembles ingredients in a serving dish.*

BILL. So you're not missing the Presidency, Roy?

ROY. You see before you a man released! Gone the perpetual to-ing and fro-ing on the Trans-Europe Express: Strasbourg, Bonn, back to Brussels, weekends at East Hendred with Jennifer, back to Brussels – Paris, of course. Gone the diplomatic summits in every European capital and some beyond – much as I relished the company of say, Helmut Schmidt, he would insist on the most thinly proportioned German vintages out of patriotic sentiment – should we even classify Riesling as a wine? The exact tincture of human urine and not a little of its taste.

DAVID. Always seemed like something of a thankless task. And where does it leave you now?

ROY. Is it not astonishing that the great privilege of leading the largest coalition of nations in history is seen by some as a bad career move? That in being at the helm of Europe I opted for a condition of semi-retirement, as if I was running a minor Oxbridge college. I never cease to despair at our parochialism – what should concern us more than Europe?

SHIRLEY. Certainly think one of the things that we all share is a passion for Europe.

ROY. True, true. Am I alone in feeling I am talking too much?

I am under-employed here. May I assist at all?

DEBBIE. In the oven, pre-heated to gas mark eight – right; thirty minutes to crisp and we can indulge in what I will call brunch.

Oh, can I take your coat, Roy?

She does.

David, has everyone got something to drink?

DAVID. Yes, more coffee on the go; tea, although it's a little early for that unless you're Wedgie Benn.

ROY. Well now, the Gang is gathered! Surely an occasion that has the savour of history; but please, do prevent me from further speechifying.

DAVID. We need to get straight down to business.

All being well we can progress this and make some moves to the press around two which might mean we can catch the dailies tomorrow.

Pause.

DEBBIE. Well, only of course if everyone agrees with that.

SHIRLEY. I for one certainly don't.

BILL. Me neither; first I've heard of it.

ROY. Yes, it does sound like something of a tight schedule, doesn't it?

SHIRLEY. What do you even intend to announce? High-level chichi lunch achieved to satisfaction of all?

DAVID. Today's the last chance to declare our hand one way or t'other. After yesterday we cannot in all honour remain in this party; which one of us can defend a union majority vote for the party leader? Defend our having less say than some beardy militant shop steward?

ROY. I count myself fortunate not to have witnessed it.

DAVID. We have the press and the country avid for us to make our move, and they won't forgive us for dithering – the nearly folk, shying at the jump – and every false start weakens us further within the party.

So I say I don't intend to stay in Labour after today.

BILL. Okay. So that's basically an ultimatum then?

SHIRLEY. For all of us it seems.

Pause.

ROY. Far be it for me to hold up your very decided plans further, David.

DAVID. Would have thought they're all our plans.

ROY. Not even any niceties… to delay them a minute or two?

DAVID. Good God, this isn't some bloody Brussels dinner party.

Awkward silence.

DEBBIE. Everyone's truly very pleased you're here, Roy. Can I maybe get you anything to drink? As David said we have coffee, tea.

ROY. I am replete. In terms of caffeinated refreshment.

DEBBIE. We so appreciate you driving here at such short notice, don't we, David?

DAVID. Yes – of course the welcome goes without saying.

ROY. In politics very little does in my experience.

Well, may we proceed without the Damoclean threat of exposure to the media at least?

DEBBIE. I think David was speaking, if I may speak for him, in hypothetical terms.

DAVID *springs into action.*

DAVID. So, fine, I'll chair then.

Debbie's kindly prepared to take minutes.

SHIRLEY. Oh. Many thanks to Debbie. For that.

DEBBIE. Apologies in advance for any misattributions.

BILL. Okay. Seems like we'd better get down to it.

ROY. A refreshing lack of ceremony I suppose.

DAVID. Have a seat. Roy, here perhaps, Shirley, okay, Bill, maybe over here – no especial significance.

SHIRLEY. Fine.

But… sorry – I'm not sure David should chair.

DAVID. Really?

SHIRLEY. No, I don't think that would work, actually. I don't know if anyone else…?

BILL. Agreed.

DAVID. What? Why the hell not, Bill?

ROY. Perhaps someone less, shall we say partisan, should take up that office.

DAVID. Who did you have in mind? Aren't we all up to our necks in this?

ROY *and* SHIRLEY *look at* BILL.

Oh, of course, the utterly pristine Bill.

BILL. I hope I am not lacking in partisan spirit.

ROY. Please don't take umbrage, David.

DAVID. I do not take umbrage whatever umbrage might be.

ROY. Yes, it's a curious word isn't it, 'umbrage'.

SHIRLEY. Bill, are you happy to do it?

BILL *grunts.*

DAVID. Outnumbered then. There are some advantages to party hierarchy I see.

Fine, fine, let's start, Bill in the bloody chair, okay.

BILL. Thank you, David, for making way with such good grace.

So we have a common understanding, at least, that we need to come up with a statement of intent in the light of yesterday?

DAVID. Stronger than that. A binding declaration to launch a new party.

BILL. Everyone happy with David's formulation of that agenda?

SHIRLEY. Not yet, no, nowhere near that.

DAVID. Not yet? When did you have in mind, Shirley?

SHIRLEY. Not as I say before we achieve a statement of common ground. Not by the way a manifesto either.

ROY. A useful distinction.

BILL. So. We seem agreed to proceed with drafting a statement of intent.

DAVID. No more hedging about. Lay the best cards now when the table is ours. In words of one syllable, are we quitting the Labour Party or not?

ROY. As someone not currently in the Labour Party I at least may be considered to be exempt from a direct answer to that.

DAVID. That's a cop-out!

BILL. Can we retain a modicum of civility?

SHIRLEY. I'm sorry but here I am with David, it is a cop-out, Roy and I think Bill, Chair, actually, right now we need to go round the table and for each one of us to come clean about who they have been talking to in the press. One by one. Precondition. And whilst we're at it perhaps it would be worth clarifying the circumstances of today, what perhaps lies behind this sudden act of largesse – because I don't know if I am alone in this but I feel however well meant, there is an agenda to all this hospitality.

DAVID. That's a time-wasting diversion, Shirley, and I must say I take issue with your unwontedly graceless reaction –

SHIRLEY. Oh is it! Well, we know who you've been talking to, plastered all over *The Sunday Times*; congratulations for your scoop, I suppose we'll boost sales tomorrow now. Perhaps that's why all of a sudden we've been summoned here to Limehouse.

DAVID. My book is an entirely separate matter, and I resent the implication…

ROY. Can I say I very much regret that this enterprise is commencing in the same rancorous spirit as a Wilson Cabinet meeting.

BILL. Second that.

SHIRLEY. Well, this is not a game… this is not Scrabble or Risk. Nor is it a smart career move. This is real, this has consequences.

DAVID. Isn't that exactly what I've been saying?

DEBBIE. David honey – sorry, just you're shouting a bit. Sorry.

Perhaps, perhaps I might speak – to the change of venue.

I've long wanted to pay you back for your kindnesses to me and David and there's such deep affinity too – between you all, I honestly think that; and if I may, I would observe this is probably not the time for habitual responses… yes, I would observe that there are maybe two questions before you, one clearly political and the other, well, personal. And I would only observe that you guys have a long personal prehistory that might sometimes get in the way of all your political futures, and bringing you here today seemed one way of maybe, well, shaking things up a little.

ROY. That's very well said, Debbie.

Pause.

DAVID. Chair, may I say some words – in my defence?

BILL. Of course. Everyone happy with that?

They all nod. DAVID *gets up and finds his papers.*

DAVID. I went into politics to change lives. In truth I dislike politics. I like action! All around us are remedies for the wrongs of this world if we could only grow up, be rational and attend to them; that's the history of my profession, medicine, that's the only reason for politics I can trust.

This time last year Shirley and Bill asked me to join the fight against the Hard Left. Roy, you'd given your Dimbleby lecture, arguing for a new party, which I took exception to, because I thought there was still hope in Labour. Jim Callaghan was a leader I could admire; Tony Benn, who I consider insane, was in the slips but not ascendant – and for all your jibes, Bill, I owe a heck of a lot to this party – youngest Health Minister, youngest Foreign Secretary; voted in four elections in a row in Plymouth, all as a Labour man!

I said the fight was *within* the party to save the party, to save the party of Europe, the party of redistributing wealth, the party, yes of the unions, but also the nation, the party that should represent the common sense of this country, and once did.

So what happened in that year?

Callaghan gave in to every demand the Left could cook up, Benn's chafing away at Deputy Leader, and we're now led by a septuagenarian happier re-reading Hazlitt than demolishing Margaret Thatcher – yes, Mrs Thatcher, despised the length and breadth of the land for runaway job losses, inflation and real pain, still sitting pretty because our voters have nowhere else to go! Because, comrades, we've failed them again and again – failed them in '64 to '70, failed them from '74 to '79 and we'll fail them even more in the unlikely event of us winning '83. The Labour Party is *decades* away from power if it even survives that long. And yet across the water in Sweden, the Netherlands, Denmark, Germany and France, social democracy thrives.

So today I changed my mind.

He gets out some copies of a memo and distributes.

Some provisional thoughts: Bill and I still have our seats – we may need to contest them, but we've got the blessings of our constituents; Shirley, you were right to step away from Stevenage as Labour, but there are towns and cities in this land avid for you to be their champion; Roy, you're a stranger to the electorate these days but you're untainted with the Callaghan years. In this document are the names of six confirmed Labour MPs prepared to cross the floor to join whatever we create here; I think if *we* jump many others will follow, because I believe there is a *massive* constituency for us out there: angry Labour voters who held their nose and voted Tory, political virgins nowhere reflected in current parties craving change, the patriotic working class sick of inane cries of 'ban the bomb' or patronising union bosses, the doctors, the teachers, the businessmen, the entrepreneurs, the many, many people of this country who deplore extremes but hunger for justice!

So yes – yes, I want us to leave this room, smash the two-party log-jam and let loose the energy of the British people.

And I simply ask, here, now: are you with me?

Silence. They contemplate his memo. The silence grows.

Well? What the hell is this?

What can be holding you people back?

ROY. Actually, David, I find little to demur from in your speech bar its excitability.

DAVID. For God's sake, Roy, need you be so damned old-school about this… where is the passion in you – Bill? Shirley?

DEBBIE. David. Calm down, love.

DAVID. Bill, you know this is a busted flush, so are you maybe what, afraid – for your prospects? Come out into the open, dukes up – certainly had you down as a fighter, Shirley, when did you get so vacillating and timid –

SHIRLEY. I can't believe I am listening to this macho – calumny.

BILL. Can we please all behave with more mutual respect?

David, would you like to sit down perhaps?

David?

DAVID *is by the window.*

SHIRLEY. We can't just be – suborned – this document is – you even specify the ruddy seats I am apparently to run for…

BILL. It's… You've certainly done your homework but…

ROY. Oh, I note we even have your thoughts about leadership specified. Good news for Shirley it seems.

SHIRLEY. It's a bloody shopping list is what it is!

DAVID. If it's so fucking objectionable for you to hear the truth then yes, fine, I suggest we agree to end this right now.

SHIRLEY. Right, okay, right, if that's where this is going, if that's the tenor –

BILL. Let's remove the personal dimension from this – set this specific –

ROY. We seem fated to misunderstand and misrepresent each other. Perhaps this meeting is premature after all.

Silence.

DEBBIE. Chair, may I…?

BILL *nods.*

Shall we set this aside for now, allow these thoughts – to percolate – create a little space, David, allow everyone a little more time… I do think we're doing all this heavy work on an empty stomach – an army marches on its stomach, right?

And I also believe we have a bottle of Château Lafite arriving at room temperature, right, Bill?

Pause.

BILL. That's absolutely right.

ROY. Did you say a Lafite?

DEBBIE. 1964 vintage.

BILL. In your honour, Roy.

ROY. 1964? A fine summer in the Bordeaux – but was it not somewhat wet in the Medoc during harvest?

DEBBIE. Actually I believe they picked the grapes a little early, escaping the unduly damp September.

ROY. Yes, that's absolutely right – 1964.

Good year; I was Minister for Aviation.

BILL. Oh, '64. My first term of Government.

SHIRLEY. Me too. MP for Hitchin.

ROY. Wilson's best years. David, I think was yet to join us.

Yes, an auspicious vintage.

I do hope it will not be opened on my account alone.

DEBBIE. Oh it's already standing wide open.

Pause.

SHIRLEY. Well, personally I'm keeping a clear head.

DAVID. Yes, I'm staying dry.

ROY. The Lafite in my experience only serves to clarify thought.

But if I am to be the only imbiber let it remain *en bouteille*.

Pause.

BILL. Oh, look, I'll take a glass with you, Roy.

DEBBIE. Me too. What the hell? I'm off-duty, right.

So here we go. So.

Roy, presumably you'll want to inspect the cork.

ROY. May I?

She hands him it; he sniffs it. ROY *takes the bouquet.*

One detects the warm soil after a summer downpour.
Mmmm. Now, I think you may pour.

DEBBIE. 'Beaker full of the warm south' for you coming up.

ROY. She's wonderfully vivacious, David.

DEBBIE. Ha!

BILL. Yes. And speaking for myself it's very, very good to
see you, Roy; to have you here amongst us; that we're all
here today.

SHIRLEY. Yes, of course, yes.

Oh, God, go on, pour me one as well, I probably need loosening up a bit.

DEBBIE. Of course, Shirley, there – you – are. Not forgetting Bill. One for me too.

David, make it a level pitch, honey?

Pause.

DAVID. Never let this be known; the press would have a field day.

DEBBIE *pours a glass for* DAVID. *All bar* DAVID *raise their glasses.*

ROY. *Santé.*

BILL. Good health.

SHIRLEY. Bottoms up!

DEBBIE. Mud in your eye?

DAVID *looking out the window out front.*

DAVID. I'll drink to Attlee not Wilson.

Lived across the street.

Brightlingsea buildings.

BILL. I'll drink to that.

They drink.

Served this constituency for thirty years.

DAVID. Absolutely. I think of him daily.

DEBBIE. Roy, didn't, didn't you know him rather well?

ROY. Indeed. My father was his Parliamentary private secretary.

SHIRLEY. Gosh, I don't know that I knew that, Roy.

ROY. The night Father died, Clem put us up in Number 10.

DAVID. Not a man of words; a doer.

ROY. Yes, yes he was.

DAVID (*joins them at the table*). Look, I recognise I am a –
hothead.

I am Welsh, in the end.

And yes, I can… overstep the mark.

I wonder if I really am suited to this game; not got the
patience in me perhaps. Too much to get done it seems to
waste time in, well – sparing feelings.

SHIRLEY. We're all rather tougher than that implies, David.

DAVID. I'm not in the business of apologies.

BILL. I don't see anyone calling for one.

Pause.

SHIRLEY. Can I perhaps respond to David? Bill?

BILL *nods.*

Our party is sick, profoundly sick, hopefully not terminally
but – well – parties can die – look what happened to the
Liberals! But if that were to happen it would put the ordinary
British working person at such grave risk.

She gulps down some wine.

Oh and I actually admire Margaret, she's got guts, fight, but
she's out of control, there's no real check on her, dead set on
laying waste to anything called socialism, something vengeful
about it, cruel about it. Watch out if you're poor, watch out if
you're in a union, just watch out – if she has her way, the
future's terrifying – she'll strip away every protection, every
law, everything commonly owned and leave us all exposed to
the most ruthless capitalism imaginable.

My God, I fear that future, a future without the Left.

But – what's so very novel about what you propose? I just
don't see it, David, this movement you invoke, this
constituency we've yet to meet, all these impatient middle-
class folk, all these harrumphing doctors and dentists and
dons so eager for us to throw our hats into the ring– I'm
sorry, all I can see is more of your sort, men of a certain age,
pale-skinned and well-heeled –

DAVID. I thought *ad hominem* ridicule was below you –

SHIRLEY. We cannot create a party without roots, a party made
for the middle class by the middle class, a party standing for
little other than its own neck and thereby in the process
destroying, yes, the very best hopes of the working class, the
party they built, which they have bequeathed to us, the
movement of hope which is finally why I'm in this game;
you see I keep channels open, I remain on good terms with
the unions.

ROY. Perhaps you are unready to hazard your popularity.

SHIRLEY. Ha! Thanks a bunch, Roy – well, let's just say I am
not persuaded that ripping up a hundred years of history is
necessary as things stand. You ought to hear that right now.
If this meeting is about deepening the fight to save true Labour
and what it stands for, yes, yes I am with you; but if it's about
wrecking it beyond recognition for some vanity project, well,
sorry, you can count me and Bill out. Right, Bill?

BILL *nods*.

So that's put a dampener on it. Sorry.

Silence. The timer goes. DEBBIE *springs up*.

DEBBIE. Looks like brunch is good to go.

So, as you know I am trialling something from one of my
clients, a certain Delia Smith; I hope everyone likes
macaroni cheese but she's classed it up a little, we have a
super-rich cheese sauce, very creamy and just a twist of
cayenne pepper, with lardons and a nice crisped-up
breadcrumb coating.

Okay, so here we go, maybe I can serve you some… up.

BILL *springs up*.

BILL. Plates are good and warm. Not to say – ouch – hot.

SHIRLEY. Look, I'll serve –

DEBBIE. No, no you stay there. I'll bring it over.

And, Roy, I'll break protocol and serve you first you've
come the furthest.

ROY. Ah – it looks very – comforting. Macaroni cheese you say?

DEBBIE. Rustic. Still a little hot. I hope you like pasta?

ROY. Andreotti always berated me for my somewhat traditional palate.

DEBBIE. Okay, well, just leave anything you –

ROY. Not at all, I will… engorge myself.

He plays with it.

DEBBIE. Okay, and Shirley, there you go.

SHIRLEY. Oh just a small helping, Debbie.

DEBBIE. A little more than that I think.

SHIRLEY. Fabulous aroma.

DEBBIE. And, Bill, you've been more than patient.

BILL. Marvellous. Anyone missing my catering?

DAVID. 'Catering' slightly flatters it.

BILL. Touché.

ROY. I always rather enjoy Bill's Marmite doorsteps.

DEBBIE. David?

DAVID. Pile it high; I am ravenous.

They eat.

SHIRLEY. God it's actually utterly – scrummy. There's cream in there?

DEBBIE. The cream's the *coup de grâce*; Delia is an utter genius.

BILL. Maybe she embodies the spirit of what we might be about. *Déclassé*, pragmatic.

DAVID. Quite so – shouldn't everyone live well? People resent being bossed around by the Galloping Gourmet and What's-her-face Craddock.

ROY. Fanny. Craddock.

Wonderfully filling.

Yes, I've always felt it was about raising all boats with the tide.

SHIRLEY. You've hardly touched it, Roy.

ROY. Somewhat… rich; I shall pick at it.

And I suspect I owe you an account of my… stance.

Chair, may I offer a response to Shirley and David?

BILL (*wiping his mouth*). Roy. Of course. (Are we allowed seconds?)

DEBBIE *nods*.

ROY. Yes, I think a little earlier I was accused of 'copping out'.

SHIRLEY. Roy, look, I take that phrase back.

ROY. Nevertheless, yes, I'd like to respond. In fact I have a larger proposition to offer.

ROY *pushes away his plate*.

Oh dear – was I six during the General Strike? Yes.

I remember little other than my father disappearing. Arrested, yes, although I didn't know that… at the time.

Arrested – at a picket line; charged with 'Illicit Assembly'.

He cleans his glasses.

DEBBIE. Sorry, Roy – just to say there's salad here and freshly baked bread. Sorry again, Roy.

ROY. Not at all.

Some so-called 'Blacklegs' refused to observe the strike, Father was a miner's agent. He went along to the picket and he maintained, even as the police charged them on horseback with batons, breaking open heads without fear or favour – Father maintained his sole wish was to prevent bloodshed.

Which seems true to the man I remember.

Nevertheless at Monmouth Assizes he was sentenced to six months imprisonment!

SHIRLEY. Disgraceful.

(Sorry, Debbie, any pepper?)

DEBBIE *passes it over.*

ROY. All of this was kept from me, from his son. The shame.

Britain – before the Labour Party's ascendancy. Maybe as
you say, Shirley, a country to which we are returning.

But – but even so, my contention is that Labour has achieved
its historical task, and must now make way for something new.

He looks around at them all and smiles. Everyone's still.

As you know I have the greatest respect for the Liberal
tradition, not the same, David, not the same as today's feeble
Liberal Party, I see you scowling, not the same in fact.

But need I remind you that the Labour Party was an outgrowth
of the Liberal Party? – that in its infancy electoral pacts were
necessary for Labour to gain any foothold in Westminster?
That its personnel were often interchangeable? Even Attlee
hailed from a Liberal household, as did Beveridge, the
architect of the Welfare State, as did Keynes upon whom we
have all so heavily relied – all Liberal, all Progressives. Why
should we lionise one voice for the Left, as if the working
people's needs took only one form? And I think I know them
as intimately as any of you might.

One tragedy of the twentieth century in my view is the entire
eclipse of the Liberals by Labour; and yet the junior party,
our party, has never – with the exception of 1945, and then in
the extreme forcing house of war – *never* commanded a
convincing majority in this country; not even I may say
within the very working classes that we apparently serve.

And I am saying that as one who came to term in the very
womb of Labour, and felt the honour of being its servant,
and for all my reserve my unwillingness to – to what – to –
say what I feel, shall we say – saying even this much is a –
stab – to the heart.

He gulps down some wine.

And whilst I know for many of you my tenure in Europe
might be deemed as, oh, what, a 'cushy number', a ringside
seat that has left me untainted by the collapse of Callaghan,
well, it may also have served to offer me a clarifying vantage
point. I have certainly come to note that no other party of the

Left has so narrowly hitched its wagon to the trade union movement, which now turns against it; I would note also that our party conducts itself more like a revivalist religious movement, with traitors and apostates, than a grown-up rational force for change – again *uniquely*.

Would it actually be possible to 'betray' the Conservative Party? Who are their traitors and rogues? Their only heresy is failure.

SHIRLEY *checks her watch – signals to* BILL. DAVID *notes this*.

BILL. Roy, we are short of time.

ROY. Thank you. Noted.

In every election since 1951, our vote has declined and our support within our constituency fallen, our party membership has withered year on year; meanwhile we have handed over power again and again to a uniquely reactionary Conservative Party, so that as nation we fall ever more behind socially, economically, culturally, that we remain obsessed with a past we can't even remember correctly, obsessed with classes that have long since passed out of observable existence, obsessed with what divides us and not what unites us, and that right now, yes, Mrs Thatcher is intent on deepening that very divide until it may not be bridged – two million out of work! Communities set adrift! Belligerent warmongering! The precious achievements we have secured, our National Health Service, our comprehensive education, our civilising trend to redistribute wealth, the post-war settlement I believe made this country happier, fairer, more at ease with itself than ever before, torn to tatters by minorities of Right and Left.

And I believe with David – I know – that the nation looks on at all this in disgust and dismay; and that out there lies a demonstrable appetite for *more* equality, *more* democracy, *more* freedom. Where else might this be created than in the centre of politics and how else without the aid of the Liberal Party even in its remnant state?

And I for one am avid to create that new politics even if it means giving up personal security, risking my reputation, ceaseless effort for very possibly very little reward.

I am, yes... as I say... avid.

So, I declare my hand.

I, like David, wish to take the fight beyond the Labour Party.

Pause.

Nor did I intend to speak at such length; for which I apologise.

BILL *claps, the others join him except for* DAVID.

DAVID. If you want to join the Liberals, Roy, I'm sure you'll be made very welcome.

ROY. I wonder why you hate the Liberals so profoundly – wasn't your mother a Liberal?

DAVID. My mother really has nothing to do with this.

ROY. I do not suggest we join the Liberals but I cannot see how we can avoid working with them. Which may, yes, involve a degree of humility and compromise.

SHIRLEY. I'm with David on this; there are nice enough folk in the Liberal Party, but I see no real hunger for change, no rage at injustice. You see them through their history and you discount Labour far too easily by the way.

ROY. Am I alone in finding all this dispiriting? Bill?

Pause.

BILL. May, may I be allowed to step away from the chair for a moment.

SHIRLEY *looks at* BILL *who doesn't return her gaze;* DAVID *at* ROY.

DAVID. Of course.

BILL. I am honoured to be in your company. I just wanted to say that.

SHIRLEY. Oh Bill –

BILL. I'm well aware I'm not in your league, any of you – fine, I'm the handmaiden rather than the event itself.

Shirley, I think we first met, 1949 – Oxford Labour Club –?

SHIRLEY. Must have been.

BILL. You were the Isis Idol, and I was what – ? Club Treasurer! Elected unopposed. None of you bright sparks would touch that task with a bargepole, I offered quite cheerfully.

DAVID. Can we cut out the fond reminiscence?

BILL. Unlike you I like politics, David – always have, yes you can denounce me as lacking in passion, rhetorical power, I wouldn't disagree – sorry, double negative – I'm well aware of my limitations and indeed the limitations of politics... and I feel so... upset... that I might – that what we are doing might be – damaging to those very fine... people –

He's tearful.

DEBBIE. Bill.

BILL. Well, he wanted passion, right?

Yes, the constituency, my union, my agent, you know I have been delighted to serve the unions, Roy, maybe we differ there, I concede they have been hijacked but to me at best they are the soul of the Labour Party, no less, and I worry we now only mention them to traduce them. They've enemies enough out there.

So yes, I go between – constituents, voters, unions, party members, the Right faction, the Liberals, the Tories even, although I'll not have them in the house – back and forth, filling up this address book with names, comrades, allies, friends – your names – rarely getting hot under the collar, never an orator, not much cop on policy – but I make politics happen! And we're going to need to be bloody good at politics to conjure a party into being – right? – building up local parties, working out what seats to contest, doing the endless calculations, working together with all sorts of strange bedfellows, David. And even now, were I to leave the party, I have in this notebook the names of eight MPs who will join us; at a stroke. Because what I despise is the opposite of politics which is in my view zealotry, and zealotry has captured the party I've served since I was sixteen and served to make mock of it.

SHIRLEY. Bill, be very careful now; you sound like you're saying you're leaving?

BILL. You only leave something if you know where you're going is worthwhile, better, not some self-congratulatory gesture.

SHIRLEY. Do you honestly think it can be more than that?

BILL. How can we know, Shirley? We're sewn in our traditions like our skin, can't see past them like we can't see through that wall, like we can't see five minutes ahead even. This is a first-past-the-post nation, two parties coming and going, forever and a day; as Roy says; has been in truth for hundreds of years. Do new parties survive – what are our precedents? The Common Wealth Party, the British Union of Fascists, the Communists – hardly encouraging! Voters tend to the centre and even if they like us, even if they like what we offer, in the polling booth they'll ask themselves the hard question: is this vote a wasted vote? And political movements don't start like this, they seep up from the ground, they're not conjured into being by high-minded folk in light-filled rooms. The Gang of Four – really! To get anywhere in this endeavour we're going to have to poach – *steal* – most, if not all of Labour's vote share – those votes won't come from nowhere; we're going to have wrench friends and colleagues from their hard-won seats, fight by-election by by-election, house to house, street to street; if we don't prevail we'll wreck our careers and we'll wreck the lives of colleagues and friends if we do – if we don't recognise the slog and the hurt ahead of us we're kidding ourselves.

We have to destroy the party that made us all – and we will be *hated* for that.

And rightly so, rightly so.

Pause.

DAVID. So fine, fine, very good – but what exactly are you saying?

BILL. I'm saying – I am just saying, David – I don't honestly know. Blame the paracetamol and the fucking – Château Lafite.

He stumbles away from the table.

DEBBIE. Bill.

Bathroom's on the right... across the...

He walks out.

DAVID. So – I am assuming that's two versus two?

Two for out but on entirely contrary terms; two to stay in for no clear reason but... sentiment.

SHIRLEY. Conviction actually.

ROY. Impasse, then. Honourable perhaps, but ineffectual.

DAVID. Hopeless. Unless, Shirley... we have you wrong.

SHIRLEY. Oh I'm absolutely with Bill I'm afraid.

ROY. Out of sheer stubbornness?

SHIRLEY. Oh dear, I think Bill said it very well – is that the time?

BILL *rushes back in.*

BILL. I am saying yes.

SHIRLEY. What?

BILL. Yes.

DAVID. 'Yes'? To what?

BILL. I am saying I can no longer imagine myself out there, on the stump, for Labour –

SHIRLEY. Bill – slow down.

BILL. I am saying sometimes you have to jump out and see where the hell you land.

I am saying that.

Pause.

DAVID. Well said, well bloody said, Bill.

ROY. Three declared, eight, maybe more to join us. Already more than Macdonald in '31. I predict we may achieve

through a multiplier effect sixty seats in 1983. If we align
with the Liberals which I know is controversial –

Yet, Shirley, you remain steadfast?

The doorbell rings.

DEBBIE. Who's that?

DAVID. I have no idea.

SHIRLEY. It's for me.

She gets up and looks out the window.

Yes.

BILL. Shirley.

DAVID. What do you mean for you?

SHIRLEY. Probably should have mentioned but I have an
interview, prior commitment. Only on the radio but there is
it, nothing to be done.

DAVID. An interview – what, what are you talking about?

SHIRLEY. I don't know how to explain it better than that, it
was in the diary – so sorry, I really have to get going.

DAVID. Shirley, no, no don't you dare. I am sorry, but don't
you dare. Did anyone know about this?

BILL. She told me. Earlier.

DAVID. She told you. And you, you didn't think to mention it?
Roy?

ROY. First I heard of it but I can't say I am surprised by it.

SHIRLEY. As I say a prior commitment, David, sorry, but there
it is.

DAVID. But to talk about what – to talk about this? Because
this is very much our business.

SHIRLEY. You know very well I don't set the media's agenda.

DAVID. You cannot mention it, you cannot even allude to it –

SHIRLEY. Are you my press secretary now? Right, I'm sorry, sorry –

ROY. You could leave us with your resolution one way or the other.

SHIRLEY. I don't care to be strong-armed –

ROY. Who here is strong-arming you?

SHIRLEY. Well, that is what I sense here even from people I imagined I respected even – loved.

BILL. You think I'm letting you down?

SHIRLEY. You're spot-on in your analysis, Bill, but way off – way off – in your conclusions.

ROY. You risk retreating into dogma –

The bell rings again.

DAVID. Ignore it, I can speak to them, it's entirely possible to defer to cancel.

SHIRLEY. Sorry, no, we go out live at 1 p.m.

DAVID. Decline to speak then, I do it all the time.

SHIRLEY. And why should I do that? You don't need me, you've all declared your stance, I remain to be convinced –

DAVID. You fought fascism in the past. You said yourself what we face is akin to that –

SHIRLEY. You will not bully me into going along with that kind of talk. I am tired of bullies, I think this is about your ambition not the party's interests.

ROY. No one is bullying anyone, we are simply seeking to persuade you to have the courage of your own convictions – we have all taken our courage from them.

SHIRLEY. No, no, I see more vanity in this than good politics, I'm sorry.

DAVID. You cannot cannot do this.

SHIRLEY. Your plans are pretty clear and I have been equally clear that I cannot support them so you'd be better off without me around.

DAVID. You cannot do this because I've called the bloody press.

Pause.

ROY. I'm sorry?

DEBBIE. David?

DAVID. Yes, I er – called the press association – earlier – and they're coming in – mmm – two hours, we need to check in but.

Yup. Whole rat pack.

ROY. But this was never agreed by us. You implied your earlier allusion was simply hypothetical.

DAVID. Okay, I set it in motion this morning because – I, I had intended if all else failed to, of course, call them off – but as we were getting somewhere – and someone's got to force the pace on this and that's exactly what I – did.

BILL. Oh my Christ.

DAVID. So you see, Shirley, if you breathe a word about this you'll steal our thunder, and if you say you're out of the Gang, we will all look utter arses, so what exactly will you say?

BILL. David, I am sorry, but that – what you did – is totally out of fucking order.

DAVID. Well that happens to be where we are, Bill, so tough titty.

SHIRLEY. I'll do what I can to limit the damage but even if I refuse to go now that would speak volumes, and do you know, actually, I don't see saving your face as my problem.

Well – this has been – memorable.

Debbie, thanks so much for brunch; all quite delicious.

DEBBIE. Sure. I'll pass that on. To Delia.

SHIRLEY *goes.*

Blackout.

The World at One *on the radio.*

Five

1 p.m. – lunch is over, radio is on a low volume; BILL *is lying on the floor whilst* ROY *sits and* DAVID *writes;* DEBBIE *sits at the typewriter. The Lafite is finished.*

DAVID. Right! How's this:

> 'It is now necessary to campaign for the values, principles and policies of social democracy within the United Kingdom.'

DEBBIE *types.*

DEBBIE. 'It… is… now… necessary… to campaign… for the… values…'

BILL. No too abstract. We need to home in on why today.

DAVID. We also need to outline what the declaration is saying.

ROY. What do you have, Bill?

BILL. Mmm:

> 'The calamitous Labour Party conference in Wembley demands a new start'?

DEBBIE. Okay: 'The calamitous… Labour Party… conference in…'

ROY. Apologies, Debbie: is that too divisive a beginning? Does it not anchor us in history too firmly?

BILL. How can we start in any other way?

ROY. Now, I have:

> 'The time has come to set up a council for social democracy.'

DEBBIE. Whoawhoawhoa… okay: 'The time has – '

ROY. 'The time has come to set up…'

DEBBIE. '…the time has come to set up a…'

ROY. '…to set up… a council for…'

DAVID. No, no, no, dull as December, half-hearted, half-baked –

ROY. I am more than happy to be criticised but not abused, David.

DAVID. We all appreciate your fine prose, Roy, but this is a manifesto –

ROY. Neither do I need your faint praise –

DAVID. This is not a memo to some bureaucrat in Brussels – this is a call to arms –

ROY. Ah, the constant rush to bellicose rhetoric –

BILL. Gentlemen, please –

ROY *gets up.*

ROY. There is so little precedent for what we are seeking to achieve. The founding of the major parties is shrouded in mystery – the Whigs and Tories seemed to arise organically; even Labour simply emerged. Yet we must invent ourselves by fiat; and I suspect our largest challenge is our entire lack of membership.

DAVID. Oh we'll acquire a membership in due course.

BILL. We don't need it in due course, we need it right now.

ROY. Not to mention a presence in the House. A mere two MPs thus far, defections aside.

DAVID. Well, doubtless someone will obligingly die soon and we can throw ourselves at a by-election.

BILL. I think in all honesty David and I should resign our seats and stand again for the new party. But I suspect I'd thereby lose my seat reducing us to a party of one.

DAVID. Nonsense – you say yourself we have MPs ready for this, Wrigglesworth, Thomas, we have Maclennan, we have the potential of what's-'is-face – Brocklebank-Fowler –

BILL. Ha! Poaching Tories now are we?

DAVID. If they sign up to what we offer, do we turn them down?

ROY. There's no alternative to forging electoral pacts – if we break bread with the Liberal Party, we can agree to contest some seats and not others –

DAVID. Ah yes, after the dazzling success of the Lib-Lab pact – brilliant.

BILL. And meanwhile we have no short money, no election war chest, no infrastructure and some of us are not even salaried –

DAVID. Can we focus on solutions rather than problems?

DEBBIE. I know a few things about the money question – if it's helpful. You draft a large ad in all the major papers; I could maybe pay for it. Then you hit every link and every friend in the media hard, and I think they'll be eating out of your hands. Then you sweat all the business links you can find and you get them to stump up upfront – because money will find money. These are really not insuperable problems.

DAVID. Right, right, and if today we all allocate roles – I can work on constitutional matters perhaps, Bill, you'd be best on recruitment, membership, shaping the party and Roy – Roy, you – well, I don't know, what do you think, fundraising?

ROY. I beg your pardon.

DAVID. Rounding up donors?

A vital role – *the* role – as we have discussed.

BILL. I hardly think that's Roy's – metier.

DAVID. Why ever not, he's in the thick of the great and the good?

ROY. I see, David! So you imagine I am the appropriate person to go around Whitehall shaking some begging bowl wooing the monied – this is how you see me? Some oily plutocrat out of Trollope.

DAVID. If you're too grand to do the necessary spadework involved, Roy, I'm happy to swap tasks with you but if we all begin so high and mighty as this then I scarcely see –

ROY. 'High and mighty' – you fling some skivying task at me then you rubbish me for my apparent reluctance to be steamrollered –

BILL. Gentlemen, please –

DEBBIE. Oh, hang on, hang on – it's on, it's now.

DAVID. If we are to get anywhere we might need to be a tad less sensitive –

ROY. I expect you'll find that rather easier than most of us –

BILL. This is us – the bloody Gang of Three.

A table with a missing leg.

DAVID. Well if you don't like it get on the phone to the BBC and get her back here.

DEBBIE. Can I just remind everyone that whatever Shirley says in that radio studio right now could wipe out anything anyone says in this room. Okay.

DEBBIE *turns up the radio; an interview with* SHIRLEY.

INTERVIEWER. My guest today is Shirley Williams, former Labour MP for Stevenage and Minister for Education; Mrs Williams, you have to agree that yesterday's conference marks a kind of new nadir for the Labour Party.

SHIRLEY. Well, it certainly felt like it at times.

DAVID. So far so good.

ROY. Sssh.

INTERVIEWER. And you are of course associated with the so-called Gang of Four – David Owen, Roy Jenkins –

SHIRLEY. And Bill Rodgers yes, well, we have never chosen that name –

BILL (*chuckles*). Nice to be remembered –

DAVID. Sssh!

INTERVIEWER. But there has been talk of leaving the Labour Party, has there not?

ROY. The moment of truth.

They all stand very quietly.

SHIRLEY. Well, I myself am not aware of any such talk.

INTERVIEWER. Really; certainly David Owen seemed to suggest otherwise – ?

DAVID. Rot!

SHIRLEY. Look I am a member of the National Executive Committee, I am a deeply loyal member of the party, with far more years to my name than some of my challengers –

ROY. Nice return slice. Just scraped the net.

INTERVIEWER. So I repeat you are utterly ruling out leaving the party?

SHIRLEY. I… I have no plans, immediate or long term –

BILL. So that's that.

INTERVIEWER. Not immediately? But not never?

SHIRLEY. I was invited here to discuss the current state of the Labour Party not defections or putative new parties.

INTERVIEWER. Of course – but some might say that any putative new party without your participation would be doomed to failure, that it might be no more than a vanity project –

SHIRLEY. People can say what they like.

INTERVIEWER. But in truth, Mrs Williams, it's hard to imagine someone such as yourself – humane, progressive, liberal-minded – remaining in the Labour Party say of Tony Benn.

SHIRLEY. Do you know I have never actually thought politics is about me – who am I? My life, my wonderful career, my glorious future – do you think your listeners are interested in any of that? Surely we're the servants of the people, nothing more.

INTERVIEWER. And regrettably there we have to end it; Shirley Williams, thank you very much.

And now we turn to America where reports of President elect Reagan –

DEBBIE *switches it off.*

DAVID. My God she's good!

BILL. I've known Shirley run widdershins around an idea in minutes.

ROY. That's the calibre of the woman.

We see now how her absence from our midst will be read.

DAVID. Well, that's where we are.

BILL. On the evidence of the last hour I'd say we're doomed to failure without her.

DEBBIE. That's absolutely right.

Suddenly she finds herself standing up.

Absolutely right – and you'd deserve to fail because frankly any modern party without a woman at the helm should be a standing joke, from now on – you should have been on your knees to her, honest to God.

DAVID. Debbie. I didn't have you down as some crude feminist.

DEBBIE. Is there any other kind in your view? I'm sorry but look at you all, caught up in turf wars before you're on the track – this was meant to be about a new politics, a new kind of party, wasn't it? If you can't persuade Shirley how can you persuade anybody else?

ROY. Debbie's right. Of all of us Shirley is the only one the public truly loves. Of all of us she's the only one who seems – well, good.

DEBBIE. That's absolutely not what I was saying.

DAVID. If she's too grand and good to make the break what are we supposed to do about that?

DEBBIE. Maybe you could value her more, maybe you could woo her –

DAVID. We've seen where wooing has got us –

BILL. Oh so have we been wooed?

ROY. Very winningly I am sure.

The telephone rings.

BILL. David, where are you going?

DAVID. What does it look like?

BILL. If that's the press what will you say?

ROY. We are not ready to go public.

BILL. You have to call them off, defer things.

DAVID. How's that going to look? I'll tell you; we'll look like exactly what we are, a bunch of lousy quitters.

He goes. The ringing ceases.

A slightly awed silence.

ROY. May I assist in clearing up?

I must warn you I am a terror for breaking things. Jennifer has lost all hope with me.

DEBBIE. We're all good I think.

BILL. Come on, I'll wash up at least.

DEBBIE. Okay. You can do the drying, Bill.

BILL *stacks the plates,* DEBBIE *runs the sink.* ROY *stands.*

Oh Roy, there's another bottle you know.

A later, cheaper vintage. '76, I think.

ROY. Ah, '76. Demise of the second Wilson Government.

Year of my failed bid for leadership.

Do you think consuming two could be seen as extravagant?

DEBBIE. Oh I'd say it's a crime not to drink it.

BILL. Drown our sorrows.

ROY *opens and pours three glasses, distributes them.*

ROY. Did I conclude my story? Father was arrested, yes. And there was an outcry, so extensive that even the much-maligned Ramsay MacDonald raised it in the House as a miscarriage of justice. And a petition of no less than thirty thousand signatures was raised for his release – and so Father was let out early; and when he came home every house in the valley, every miner and every miner's wife, hailed and cheered his return.

Naturally I had no idea what the commotion was about solidarity!

DEBBIE. That's truly a wonderful story, Roy.

BILL. And a salutary one.

Everyone stares into their drinks.

DEBBIE. We had miners here. I mean… in this house.

Oh gosh, where were they from?

BILL. Miners in Limehouse?

ROY. Wasn't aware of any coal deposits in the Thames Basin.

DEBBIE. Oh no, no, they were – picketing? – picketing this old coal-fired power station right across the street, closed down now. Your, your good health, gentlemen.

BILL. Indeed.

ROY. It only improves with acquaintance.

DEBBIE. Mmm, day like today, frozen – ten years ago, no – '72?

BILL. Bitterly cold winter as I recall.

ROY. Delighted not to have been Home Secretary then.

DEBBIE. Standing across the street there all day long, below-zero temperatures – I made them mugs of hot tea; too weak, no one complained, but – cupped their calloused hands round the mugs, right, right there in that doorway; like they were serfs; so who was I – Lady Muck?

I said come on in, use the facilities, the telephone – gosh, were they embarrassed, I had to insist – living out of this van, positively *arctic* in there – twelve guys from – from Nottinghamshire? – pathetically thin blankets; and it was David, yes, David who said we have to let them sleep in here, floor of the spare room. Next morning they taught me how to do a proper fry-up. Heavy on the lard. Such gentlemen; considerate, polite – as they left the shop steward made a speech… found out Attlee lived nearby, starting hymning him, saying David was his heir.

I guess he wouldn't say that now.

Pause.

ROY. Debbie, I fear I may have drunk a little too much to drive home; would you be so kind as to book me a taxi?

DEBBIE. Of course; in due course?

ROY. As soon as possible, I think.

DEBBIE. Oh. You're not staying then?

ROY. To what end?

DEBBIE. Right. Right, of course, I see.

Okay, I'll book you something; to your London place?

ROY *nods. She goes.*

BILL. How long's it take to drive from Broadcasting House to here?

ROY. She won't return.

The choice for Shirley isn't whether to stay in the Labour Party or leave; the choice for Shirley is whether to remain in politics altogether.

BILL. Yeah. Sometimes wonder if I've not carried a candle for her for thirty years.

BILL *laughs, as does* ROY.

ROY. Haven't we all? She embodies all that is best about this movement.

ROY *stands.*

I would have liked to permit myself to be excited about today; so close to the blessed goal and yet the ball goes shy! Jennifer said last night she couldn't recall me being this animated since the European referendum.

BILL. Might be a blessing – no going back to the electorate again – the sheer bloodiness of that.

ROY. You're not implying I'm past it?

BILL. Never.

ROY. You know what he said to me when I went to Europe? Our esteemed host?

'You're finished.' That's what he said to me.

BILL. Extraordinary cheek. Thinks he's Devon's JFK.

They laugh.

Everyone who has witnessed you close to loves you, Roy.
Truly you have civilised this movement, this nation.

ROY. Kind words, Bill, and welcome ones.

It's a curious life, politics; what do we leave behind us?

Do we not squander our lives in wrangling, plotting,
a thousand ephemeral gestures – like some attenuated
cricketer waiting all his days in the pavilion for the odd
short-lived innings?

I've never been at home in the Labour Party and yet it has
been my home... I had hoped this endeavour might yield the
one chance in my life when I could inhabit a movement that
is intimately connected to whom I happen to be.

But there it is.

DAVID *re-enters in a suit looking very smart, doing up a tie.*

BILL. You're looking very debonair, David.

ROY. Off to a society wedding?

ROY *and* BILL *chuckle.*

DAVID. It's for the photographers actually – they'll be here
imminently. And I made clear we won't do interviews, we
would offer up at most a written statement – no more than that.

BILL. 'Imminently'?

DAVID. Yes – oh and Debbie's typing up the declaration.

ROY. We've barely agreed the first sentence.

DAVID. Well; there we are, this forces our hand one way or...

The doorbell rings. They look at each other.

Oh. Sooner than I thought.

DEBBIE (*off*). I'll get it.

BILL. There's cars pulling up.

DAVID. They're early, then.

BILL. Yup – here they come, cameras at the ready.

DAVID. Yes, yes. My God.

ROY. David, this is not the time I know but I feel bound to say I regret very much that I cannot be associated –

DEBBIE *walks in with* SHIRLEY.

She takes them in.

SHIRLEY. So you broke open another bottle without me? Downright cheek!

She laughs; so do they.

DEBBIE. You're more than welcome to join us.

SHIRLEY. Not sure that's a good idea.

Suddenly panicked in the interview: was I tipsy? God, stewed and tongue-tied and tired.

Never drink before lunch! Hope I didn't come across as a lush?

So come on, what have I missed: did you write the manifesto? I wondered if we should call it the Limehouse Declaration?

DAVID. That certainly sounds… apt.

BILL. Catchier than the Kentish Town Declaration.

ROY. So it begins: 'The calamitous outcome of the Labour Party Wembley conference necessitates –

DAVID. Demands –

ROY. – demands a new start in British politics.'

ROY *looks to* DAVID.

DAVID. Yes, it continues: 'A handful of trade union leaders can now determine –

SHIRLEY. Dictate?

DAVID (*to* BILL). Dictate, yes, the choice of a future Prime Minister'.

BILL (*to* SHIRLEY). It goes on to say:'The conference disaster is the culmination of a long process by which the Labour Party has moved steadily away from its origins in – '

SHIRLEY. Its roots.

BILL. Yes. 'Its roots – in the people of this country.'

SHIRLEY. Well, I don't have a problem with any of that I must say.

DEBBIE. Great – so I'm taking this down, right?

DAVID. Yes. Could you, Debbie?

ROY. With some thoughts on the economy and Europe I have here.

DAVID. And on NATO, industrial policy and the like.

DEBBIE. Wonderful; I'll work up a draft – six hundred words.

She takes their notes, goes.

BILL. Why did you come back?

SHIRLEY. God knows – all those blumming questions, questions coming at me and I could only see your faces – imagining you listening in this room, wishing I was here rather than in a dungeon in Broadcasting House – amongst friends, if I may call you that; and I had this image of us going forth, so very clearly – and then I could see my father and my mother… and somehow I felt they might approve.

ROY. I believe they would.

SHIRLEY. Yes, Roy. And that maybe we aren't destroying a tradition here, maybe we're renewing it – maybe the Left's not about famous names, personalities, labels, it's about hope, a tough sort of hope for everyday justice not for some damned heaven in the never-never you have to clamber over the dead to get to. The Labour Party's the house hope built for us, oh we've been happy there – but we've outgrown it, it's too full of memory blunting us, blinding us to what's outside – and for God's sake sometimes you have to leave home!

The doorbell again.

DAVID. That'll be them.

SHIRLEY. We don't have a name!

We'll need a name at least, won't we? I bet you didn't discuss that?

ROY. Oddly enough that question has eluded us.

BILL. Gosh, yes, that's a big 'un.

Doorbell.

DEBBIE (*off*). I'll get it.

DAVID. A link with Labour might be helpful.

SHIRLEY. You don't think there's legal implications?

DAVID. I had been thinking perhaps something like: 'Social Democratic Labour'?

Pause.

BILL. 'Social Democratic Labour.'

DAVID. Yah. What do you think?

ROY. 'Social Democratic Labour.'

SHIRLEY. 'Social Democratic Labour.' Nope, don't like it.

DAVID. Yes, it's utterly shit, isn't it? How could I have even – ?

BILL. I wondered about something like 'New Labour' – to stress those continuities?

ROY. 'New Labour'?

BILL. Yes. As if we are the party, as if we never left we simply reformed.

DAVID. 'New Labour.' Mmm. Not bad.

ROY. No. Banal.

I actually thought 'Social Democrats' – to link it to our sister parties.

SHIRLEY. 'Social Democrats'… mmm. Okay. It's not awful at least.

DEBBIE *re-enters*.

DEBBIE. So they say it's too small in here, they say they need to get more context, more backdrop. So I suggested you walk over to the Basin.

DAVID. Brilliant. There's a bridge there we could stand on, it'll look – fresh.

SHIRLEY. Yes, it is rather bourgeois in here.

DEBBIE (*laughs*). Excuse me – 'bourgeois'? In what way?

SHIRLEY. Oh come on, Debbie, we're not launching an interior decorating firm.

DEBBIE. I'm deciding not to take offence at that.

BILL. Umbrage.

ROY. I expect they'll want it in daylight.

DAVID. I thought: 'put on a suit'. I suppose it's not obligatory. Backdrop of Dockland urban decay, us smart and ready for a fight.

SHIRLEY. I'm not dressed for that, I threw this on, this blouse is terrible, frumpy. The trouser suit –

DEBBIE. Maybe a change of blouse.

BILL. Am I perhaps underdressed?

ROY. Do you have a suit to hand, Bill?

BILL. I'd have to drive back to Kentish Town.

DAVID. I suppose I might have something –

BILL. No, you're bigger than me; I'd look ridiculous in your suit, David. I'd look like a pissed clown or something.

DAVID. Right now you look like a sociology lecturer.

BILL. So be it. They can take me as I am.

DEBBIE. I'll get you a blouse, Shirley.

SHIRLEY. Oh gosh, could you, Debbie?

DEBBIE. I know the very thing.

DEBBIE *goes off.* DAVID *at the window.*

BILL. If I even borrowed a tie. Shirt's got one of those floppy collars. Very fashionable in 1978. Like me.

He giggles.

Do you think we'll appear drunk? I confess I'm pretty squiffy.

DAVID. Look at that. Must be forty of the bastards. *Mail*, *Express*, *Guardian*, *Telegraph*. As if they were waiting for this.

ROY. Well, they were primed as we know.

Pause.

SHIRLEY. In the cab here, all I could think about was us in the conference hall, hand in hand, thousands of people singing, singing that song I refused to sing:

'It well recalls the triumphs past,
It gives the hope of peace at last;
The banner bright, the symbol plain,
Of human right and human gain.'

They all look at each other.

ROY. 'Though cowards flinch and traitors sneer'; always gives me the shivers.

Pause.

BILL. 'It witnessed many deed and vow
We must not change its colour now.'

Ouch.

DAVID. 'Come dungeons dark or gallows grim – '

SHIRLEY. 'It waved above our infant night
When all ahead seemed dark and… '

Silence.

She sings.

'So raise the scarlet standard high
Beneath its shade we'll live and die – '

They all join in.

ALL. 'Though cowards flinch and traitors sneer
We'll keep the red flag flying here.'

Silence. DEBBIE *comes in with a blouse.*

DEBBIE. How's this?

SHIRLEY. Ah, that's perfect. Excuse me, no looking everyone.

Debbie, would you mind...?

She turns from us, changes to hide her tears. The others look away.

The doorbell rings again. SHIRLEY*'s changed.*

DAVID. Okay.

They won't wait any longer.

SHIRLEY. What do we do now?

DAVID. Walk out, head down.

ROY. Friendly.

SHIRLEY. Yes. As if we had some wonderful secret to disclose.

BILL. No way back from here.

DAVID. No way back.

They all shake hands and kiss or hug. They leave DEBBIE.

She looks out onto the street; the sound of press bawling questions, cameras, 'Dr Owen', Mr Jenkins', 'Mrs Williams', 'Mr Rodgers'.

She suddenly gets the giggles; she's drunk.

DEBBIE. We read things through how they play out.

What if there'd been no Falklands War and the SDP'd stormed the nation in '83? Even then we got a quarter of the vote!

What if Shirley had stepped up to the plate and led instead of Roy?

What if what if what if?

The SDP crashed out by the nineties – I was probably their last member; Labour rallied. And '83 saw the election of a young lawyer – Anthony Charles Lynton Blair.

So what was that day in January about? An ectopic pregnancy? Another middle-class luncheon club between four ill-assorted misfits?

Five I should say.

I only know the biggest business these days in Limehouse is high-end estate agents and that we can't see the sky for banks and condos and that the Gang if they're alive are all old and Lib Dems or politically homeless, and that Labour's once again a minority activity and that Europe's slipping away and the Right are everywhere – everywhere – on the march.

So yes – I guess we have to ask again:

What if?

Blackout.